THE JUST SAY NO INITIATIVE

The Official Guidebook: A Life-Changing Movement to Save a Generation

By James R. Manning

2. Copyright Page

(You can adjust this based on how you want to register it, but here's a suggested version.)

© 2025 James R. Manning. All rights reserved.

No part of this book may be reproduced or used in any manner without written permission from the author, except for brief quotations used for critical review or educational purposes.

Published by [Your Publishing Name or Self-Published]
Printed in the United States of America

ISBN
Cover Design: My ChatGPT

For more information, visit: [Insert your official site or platform]

Scripture quotations are from the King James Version (KJV), which is in the public domain.

Dedication Page (Optional but powerful)

> Dedicated to the sons and daughters who have not yet discovered who they are…
And to the mothers, fathers, and leaders who refuse to let them be

Acknowledgments Page (Optional)

I would like to thank those who have stood with me in prayer and purpose through the years — especially those who believe, even when others cannot yet see. Your faith has watered this seed.

Introduction

By James R. Manning

There is a battle taking place.

Not one fought with tanks or bombs — but with silence, confusion, and fear.

As fentanyl and drug addiction sweep through our neighborhoods, far too many have accepted the lie that we are powerless. But I believe differently. I believe in the power of truth. I believe in the power of purpose. And I believe in the power of a community that refuses to remain silent.

This book is not just a manual — it is a call to rise.

It is a torch passed to those who care, who see, and who are willing to stand.

Whether you are a parent, a pastor, a teacher, or simply someone who refuses to lose another child — this book is for you.

I offer it as both a blueprint and a beacon.

May this work not just inform you — but ignite you.

Let's begin.

— James R. Manning

CHAPTER 1 — THE BATTLE WE FACE

A Crisis That Will Not Wait

We are living in a time unlike any other. What once hid in the shadows now walks openly in our streets. A silent war is taking place, one that does not fire bullets but claims lives in quiet homes, school bathrooms, parks, and bedrooms. This is the fentanyl epidemic — a deadly poison, spreading faster than many even realize.

Fentanyl is not like the drugs of yesterday. This synthetic opioid is up to 50 times stronger than heroin and 100 times stronger than morphine. It takes only a speck — barely enough to cover the tip of a pencil — to kill a person. Many who take it never intended to, because fentanyl is often mixed secretly into other drugs, pills, or even vaping products.

It has reached our youth. Our sons and daughters, many as young as middle school, are being exposed. What starts as experimentation can end in tragedy. And the danger is not just for the addicted — it is for the curious, the pressured, the misinformed.

This Is Not Just A Drug Problem — It Is A War Over Purpose

The fentanyl crisis is not only physical. It is spiritual. Behind every overdose is a stolen destiny, a life that was created for purpose and light, now caught in the grip of darkness and destruction.

Drugs rob more than health; they rob identity. They confuse the mind, weaken the will, and separate individuals from the truth of who they were created to be.

This is why The Just Say No Initiative was born.
This is not simply a drug education program — it is a life movement.
It is about preserving identity, restoring purpose, and protecting generations.

A Generation That Needs a Voice

Many parents, schools, and communities feel overwhelmed. Some have given up, thinking there is no way to stop what is happening. But giving up is not an option. Silence will not save our children. Fear will not stop the epidemic. But truth, love, and the courage to stand will.

The Just Say No Initiative gives parents, teachers, churches, and youth leaders a clear blueprint to stand in the gap.
It gives young people the power to make decisions before the crisis ever touches them.
It turns passive communities into active movements of light.

This is the battle we face.

But the good news is:
This battle can be won.

Not by human wisdom alone.
Not by government programs alone.
But by communities who rise together, under God, with one heart, one voice, and one truth.

"Arise, shine; for thy light is come, and the glory of the LORD is risen upon thee."
— Isaiah 60:1

CHAPTER 2 — THE POWER OF NO

The Gift Every Human Possesses

From the moment God breathed life into man, He gave him something extraordinary:
the power to choose.

Every human being, no matter their age, background, or circumstance, carries this gift.

The ability to say Yes or No is one of the most powerful forces given to man.

It is not just a response — it is an act of dominion.

The Just Say No Initiative is built upon this foundation:

> You do not have to be a victim of the world around you.
You can say no.

Saying No Is an Act of Strength

In a world that constantly pressures young people to fit in, to experiment, to follow the crowd — saying "No" may seem weak to some. But in truth, it is one of the strongest things a person can do.

It takes strength to say No when others say Yes.

It takes strength to walk away when others give in.

It takes strength to stand alone, knowing you are protecting your future.

Saying "No" is not about missing out — it's about holding on.
Holding on to your identity.
Holding on to your future.
Holding on to your God-given purpose.

No Is Not Negative — It Is Protective

The world often paints "No" as harsh or limiting.
But a wise "No" is a fence that guards the garden of your life.

A parent says "No" to protect a child from harm.

A leader says "No" to protect a people from danger.

A young person says "No" to protect the seed of their destiny.

When you say "No" to drugs, you are saying "Yes" to life.

The Power of No Starts Before the Temptation

One of the secrets of this Initiative is teaching young people to make the decision before the moment of pressure comes.

When you wait until you are standing at the door of temptation, the battle is harder.

But when you have already decided, long before the offer comes, your "No" is rooted, strong, unshakable.

The Just Say No Initiative teaches:

> Decide now.

Plant your "No" deep inside your heart before the trial comes.

A Spiritual Stand

At its core, every "No" to evil is a "Yes" to God.

It is not spoken alone — Heaven stands with every young person who chooses light over darkness.

> "Resist the devil, and he will flee from you." — James 4:7

This is not about human willpower alone.

It is about standing in the strength of the One who gives purpose and life.

The Seed of a Movement

When one young person says "No," others take courage.

One life inspires another.

One stand becomes a movement.

One movement becomes a city of light.

This is how communities are transformed — not by force, but by multiplied choices of truth.

The Power of No is the foundation of freedom.

It is the starting point of this entire movement.
It is the voice every child, every parent, every leader must find.

"Choose you this day whom ye will serve... but as for me and my house, we will serve the Lord."
—Joshua 24:15

CHAPTER 3 — THE VISION OF THE JUST SAY NO INITIATIVE

A City on a Hill

Every great work begins with a vision — a picture seen before it is seen.

The Just Say No Initiative was not born simply to fight drugs.

It was born to restore identity, rebuild communities, and raise up a generation that knows who they are.

At its heart, this movement is a city on a hill — a place where light shines in the darkness, where families are strengthened, and where young people walk boldly into their future.

> "Ye are the light of the world. A city that is set on an hill cannot be hid." — Matthew 5:14

This is not a temporary program. It is the planting of something permanent.

A people.

A culture.

A testimony.

Not Just Prevention — But Purpose

Many programs aim only to stop behavior.
The Just Say No Initiative goes deeper.

We are not here to simply say, "Don't use drugs."

We are here to say, "You were born for something greater."

**When people understand who they are,
the wrong choices lose their power.**

The Initiative teaches:

Identity before temptation.

Purpose before pressure.

Vision before destruction.

**We do not just pull people out of the water —
we build bridges so they never fall in.**

A Movement That Belongs to the People

One of the most powerful aspects of this Initiative is that it belongs to the community.

Parents lead.

Churches lead.

Schools lead.

Young people lead.

Law enforcement, health professionals, coaches — all have a seat at the table.

This is not a government program.
This is not a political tool.
This is a kingdom work — led by everyday people who refuse to lose another child.

The Just Say No Initiative empowers local communities to rise and take responsibility.

A Work That Multiplies

This movement is designed to grow naturally.

One city begins.

Another hears.

Leaders are trained.

Teams are formed.

New cities are launched.

Just as a seed produces after its own kind, this movement is built to multiply without losing its heart.

Every community that plants this Initiative plants a permanent light in their city.

The Strength Is in the Simplicity

The enemy works through confusion and complexity.

The Just Say No Initiative is not complicated:

The truth is simple.

The steps are clear.

The vision is pure.

Simplicity allows it to spread.
Simplicity allows it to endure.
Simplicity allows ordinary people to do extraordinary things.

The Vision in One Sentence:

> To establish permanent communities of light, where truth reigns, identity is restored, and young people are empowered to say No to destruction and Yes to their God-given purpose.

This is the vision. This is the call. This is the work before us.

CHAPTER 4 — THE 15-STEP BLUEPRINT FOR LAUNCHING THE MOVEMENT

This chapter lays out the practical steps to move from vision to reality.

If you follow these steps carefully, you will not only start a program — you will plant a living movement that will stand and grow.

FOUNDATION STAGE: PREPARATION

STEP 1 — KNOW THE VISION

Before you begin, be settled in your heart that this is not a temporary work.

- This is a permanent stand for your community.
- This is a calling, not simply a project.
- You are planting something that can remain long after you.

You must first see the vision before you can lead others into it.

STEP 2 — SECURE PERSONAL COMMITMENT

You, as the founder or leader, must commit fully to:

- Truth
- Integrity
- Compassion
- Consistency
- Listening and learning

This work requires a steady hand, a tender heart, and an unwavering mind.

STEP 3 — ASSEMBLE A SMALL CORE TEAM

No movement is built alone.
Gather 3–5 people who:

- Share the vision.
- Have clean character.
- Are willing to serve.
- Bring different skills: administration, teaching, mentoring, youth work, outreach.

Your core team is your **first circle of strength**.

STRUCTURE STAGE: ORGANIZING THE MOVEMENT

STEP 4 — DEVELOP THE PROGRAM OUTLINE

Use the following simple framework for your sessions:

1. **The Fentanyl Crisis: The Hidden War**
2. **Understanding Addiction: The Power of Influence & Choice**
3. **Identity and Purpose: Who Am I? Why Am I Here?**
4. **Family & Community Bonds: Creating Accountability**
5. **The Power of Saying No: Real-Life Training**
6. **Community Rally: Public Stand for Change**

Each lesson is short, clear, and interactive.
The power is in the discussion, not just the lecture.

STEP 5 — ESTABLISH YOUR MEETING LOCATION

Secure a consistent meeting space:

- Church fellowship halls
- Community centers
- School classrooms (after hours)
- Libraries or youth centers

Choose a place that is easily accessible and neutral for all community members.

STEP 6 — PREPARE MATERIALS

Gather your teaching materials:

- Handouts
- Testimonies
- Videos (optional)
- Personal stories
- Statistics (simple, clear)

You may also use:

- Excerpts from your book *Just Say No: Fentanyl Epidemic - A Fight for Their Future*
- Community health resources

STEP 7 — BRANDING & IDENTITY

Create a simple public image for your group:

- Logo (optional)
- Slogan: *"Just Say No — A Fight for Their Future"*
- Flyers
- Social media pages (Facebook, Instagram)
- Business cards for awareness

Consistency builds credibility.

LAUNCH STAGE: GOING PUBLIC

STEP 8 — BEGIN SMALL GROUP MEETINGS

Before going public, practice with your core team.

- Go through each session.
- Allow feedback.
- Adjust your delivery.

This creates confidence before the public launch.

STEP 9 — LAUNCH THE PUBLIC CAMPAIGN

Organize a launch event:

- Invite local officials, pastors, teachers, police, and parents.
- Share testimonies.
- Present the vision.
- Offer sign-up opportunities for families and youth.

Your launch creates the first momentum.

STEP 10 — WEEKLY SESSIONS

Run your six-session program consistently:

- Weekly or bi-weekly meetings.
- Keep sessions clear and on time.
- Encourage open dialogue.
- Build relationships.

Consistency builds trust.

SUSTAINABILITY STAGE: BUILDING LONG-TERM IMPACT

STEP 11 — FORM SUPPORT NETWORKS

As your movement grows, form support structures:

- Parent groups.
- Youth mentoring circles.
- Accountability partners.
- Family follow-up teams.

The strength is not in the event, but in the relationships that are built.

STEP 12 — MEASURE PROGRESS

Track your progress:

- Attendance growth.
- Stories of changed lives.
- Feedback from families.
- Community partnerships.

Adapt when needed — always stay true to the core vision.

STEP 13 — EXPAND TO OTHER CITIES

Once stable, train others:

- Share your story.
- Mentor new leaders.
- Use this same blueprint.

Each new city becomes another light on the hill.

GOVERNANCE STAGE: SPIRITUAL & COMMUNITY COVERING

STEP 14 — APPOINT AN OVERSIGHT COUNCIL

Form a small board of trusted elders and advisors who:

- Provide spiritual covering.
- Offer counsel and wisdom.
- Hold leaders accountable.
- Guard the purity of the vision.

STEP 15 — ALWAYS STAY TRUE TO THE PURPOSE

The greatest threat to any movement is mission drift.

- Do not allow politics, money, or outside agendas to take over.
- Stay focused: this is about **saving lives and preserving purpose**.

"Except the Lord build the house, they labour in vain that build it." — Psalm 127:1

These 15 steps are your map.
Walk them prayerfully.
Walk them carefully.
Walk them boldly.

You will not walk alone.

CHAPTER 5 — THE HEART OF THE LEADER

Before There Is Leadership, There Must Be Heart

The success of The Just Say No Initiative does not rest on the size of the crowd or the power of the speaker.

It rests on the heart of the leader.

Programs may come and go.

Crowds may rise and fall.

But the heart of the leader determines whether the light remains.

Leadership Is First Personal, Then Public

Before you lead others, you must be led yourself.

Led by truth.

Led by love.

Led by purpose.

Led by the Spirit of God.

You do not need to be a perfect person to lead. But you must be a surrendered person.

> "Search me, O God, and know my heart: try me, and know my thoughts." — Psalm 139:23

The Leader Is a Servant First

Leadership in this movement is not about position — it is about responsibility.

You are not called to rule over people.

You are called to stand with people.

You are called to serve, to lift, to protect, to guide.

The leader kneels first, so others may stand.

The Leader Must Walk in Compassion and Courage

There will be moments of pain:

Families broken by addiction.

Parents weeping over lost children.

Youth battling temptation.

Critics who misunderstand your work.

The leader does not turn away from pain.
He faces it with compassion — but also with courage.

Compassion draws near.

Courage does not compromise.

You must speak truth even when others prefer comfort.
You must love even when others turn away.
You must stand even when others sit.

The Leader Must Be Steady

Movements face waves:

Some will join.

Some will leave.

Some will praise.

Some will oppose.

The leader's heart must remain steady — not ruled by excitement or by discouragement.

Your steadiness gives confidence to others.

Your faithfulness becomes the anchor of the movement.

The Leader Is a Listener

Leaders do not assume they know everything.

Listen to parents.

Listen to youth.

Listen to your team.

Above all, listen to the Spirit of God.

Many problems are solved not by speeches, but by listening.

>Wherefore, my beloved brethren, let every man be swift to hear, slow to speak, slow to wrath: James 1:19

"He that hath an ear, let him hear what the Spirit saith unto the church." — Revelatio

The Leader Must Guard the Vision

You have been entrusted with something holy.

Guard the purity of the message.

Refuse to allow politics, money, or popularity to corrupt the work.

Keep the focus always on:

Protecting young people.

Restoring families.

Glorifying God.

The Leader Must Multiply

Your goal is not to be the only leader.
Your goal is to raise other leaders.

Train others.

Share responsibility.

Build teams that can carry the work long after you.

**The greatest leader leaves a work that
does not need him to survive.**

> "The things that thou hast heard of me... commit thou to faithful men, who shall be able to teach others also." — 2 Timothy 2:2

The Heart of the Leader Is the Heart of the Movement

If your heart stays right —
The movement will stay right.

If your heart remains pure —
The light will not be hidden.

If your heart remains surrendered —
The Spirit of God will do what no program can ever do.

"Create in me a clean heart, O God; and renew a right spirit within me." — Psalm 51:10

-

CHAPTER 6 — FREQUENTLY ASKED QUESTIONS

In every city, church, school, and home where the Just Say No Initiative is introduced, questions arise. This chapter answers some of the most common questions in a simple, clear, and truthful way.

Q1 — Is This Just Another Anti-Drug Program?

A:
No. This is not simply a drug prevention program.
The Just Say No Initiative is a movement of identity, purpose, and community restoration. While it boldly confronts the dangers of fentanyl and drug use, its core mission is to:

Equip youth with a clear sense of purpose.

Strengthen family and community bonds.

Teach young people to make strong decisions before temptation arises.

Build long-term accountability structures, not short-term programs.

Q2 — Who Can Lead a Just Say No Initiative Group?

A:

Any person who:

Understands the vision.

Is willing to serve.

Has a clean and upright life.

Can work with both youth and adults.

Is teachable, humble, and submitted to the Spirit of God.

You do not need a professional counseling license or advanced degrees. This movement is built for ordinary people who carry an extraordinary burden to protect this generation.

Q3 — Can Churches Be Involved?

A:
Absolutely.
Churches are natural and powerful partners for this Initiative.

They offer locations for meetings.

They provide spiritual covering.

They supply leadership, counseling, and prayer.

This movement does not replace the role of the church — it often flows directly out of it.

Q4 — Can Schools Be Involved?

A:
Yes — many schools welcome initiatives that help students face the real dangers they encounter.

Sessions may be offered as after-school programs.

Parent and teacher groups may form as support teams.

School resource officers may participate.

Always approach schools respectfully, presenting the purpose and structure clearly.

Q5 — Is This a government or Political Program?

A:
No.
This movement does not belong to any government or political agenda.

It is a community-led and faith-driven work.

It welcomes partnerships, but it remains independent.

Its message is centered on truth, not on political debates.

This allows the work to remain pure, focused, and unchanging.

In this movement government officials are one of the people; and as one of the people they have a place at the roundtable.

Q6 — What Age Group Is This For?

A:
The core focus is youth — primarily ages 10 to 18. However:

Parents of younger children are encouraged to start early teachings.

College-aged youth can also benefit.

Adult support groups, parents, and leaders are fully involved in the process.

The earlier young people are exposed to truth and purpose, the stronger their decisions will be when faced with pressure.

Q7 — What About Youth Already Struggling with Drugs?

A:
The Initiative welcomes those who are struggling.
It offers:

A safe place to hear truth without judgment.

Accountability and mentorship.

Referral connections for professional counseling or medical

treatment when needed.

However, this is not a medical treatment program. It is a prevention, intervention, and restoration movement that works best when partnered with proper medical or counseling services when necessary.

Q8 — Is There a Cost to Join?

A:
There is no charge for young people or families to participate.

The Initiative operates through volunteer leadership.

Local communities may raise funds for materials, space rental, and events.

No one is denied participation based on finances.

The work is accessible to all.

Q9 — How Long Does the Program Last?

A:
The initial program is structured in six sessions.
However, the true strength of the Initiative is in the ongoing relationships that continue after the sessions.

Support groups.

Mentoring circles.

Family accountability partnerships.

The RoundTable is for everyone where the whole community

benefits.

The movement is designed to remain a permanent part of the community's life.

Q10 — What If I Feel Unqualified to Lead?

A:
You are not alone. Many great leaders start by feeling unqualified.
But remember:

This is not about perfection — it's about availability.

If your heart is pure and your motive is right, God will supply what you lack. In truth He can change even your heart and its motives.

Training materials, team support, and step-by-step guidance are provided.

> "Faithful is He that calleth you, who also will do it." — 1 Thessalonians 5:24

And I thank Christ Jesus our Lord, who hath enabled me, for that he counted me faithful, putting me into the service; 1 Timothy 1:12

CHAPTER 7 — CLOSING WORDS OF ENCOURAGEMENT

The Light Is Stronger Than the Darkness

You have seen the crisis.
You have received the vision.
You have been given the steps.
And now, you are called to the work.

This movement was never intended to be built by the powerful, the rich, or the famous.

It is built by ordinary people who carry an extraordinary burden — people like you.

The fentanyl epidemic is not the final word over this generation.

The enemy is strong, but the Light is stronger.

> "And the light shineth in darkness; and the darkness comprehended it not." — John 1:5

You Are Planting More Than a Program

When you launch a Just Say No Initiative group, you are not simply starting a class.

You are planting:

A place of safety for children.

A gathering of truth for families.

A shelter for those who are tempted.

A fortress for those who have fallen.

You are building a city on a hill — one that cannot be hidden.

You Are Not Alone

Though the work may feel heavy at times, remember:

Others are rising with you.

Communities across the country will stand shoulder to shoulder with you.

Most importantly — God is with you.

> "Fear thou not; for I am with thee: be not dismayed; for I am thy God: I will strengthen thee; yea, I will help thee; yea, I will uphold thee with the right hand of my righteousness." — Isaiah 41:10

The Seed You Plant Will Outlive You

You may never see the full harvest of the work you begin.
But long after you have finished your part, the light you plant today will continue shining.

A child who says "No" today may become a leader tomorrow.

A family restored today may heal generations to come.

A city awakened today may influence entire regions.

This is how the Kingdom of God advances — one seed, one soul, one stand at a time.

The Final Call

Do not delay.

Do not fear.

Do not wait for perfect conditions.

Begin.
Plant the vision where you stand.
The movement has already begun — and you are part of it.

> "Arise, shine; for thy light is come, and the glory of the LORD is risen upon thee." — Isaiah 60:1

APPENDIX — TOOLS FOR LAUNCHING YOUR JUST SAY NO INITIATIVE

A. SAMPLE FLYER TEMPLATE

JUST SAY NO INITIATIVE
"A Fight for Their Future"

Community Launch Meeting — All Are Welcome

Date: [Insert Date]

Time: [Insert Time]

Location: [Insert Location]

Contact: [Phone / Email / Website]

Our Mission:
To protect our children, strengthen our families, and build a permanent community of light that stands against drug abuse, addiction, and destruction.

This is more than a program — it's a movement.

Real Truth

Real Support

Real Community

Come and learn how you and your family can be part of the solution.

"The light shines in the darkness, and the darkness has not overcome it." — John 1:5

B. PLEDGE CARD TEMPLATE

JUST SAY NO INITIATIVE PLEDGE CARD

I, _____,
choose to stand for truth, for life, and for my future.

I will say NO to drugs, fentanyl, and all substances that destroy life.

I will say YES to purpose, truth, and my God-given identity.

I will protect my life, my family, and my community.

Signed: _____
Date: _____

> "Choose you this day whom ye will serve..." — Joshua 24:15

C. SAMPLE WEEKLY SCHEDULE

SESSION 1 — The Fentanyl Crisis: The Hidden War

Introduce the danger and reality of fentanyl.

Testimonies and facts.

SESSION 2 — Understanding Addiction: The Power of Influence & Choice

What addiction is.

How choices shape life.

SESSION 3 — Identity and Purpose: Who Am I? Why Am I Here?

Teaching on personal identity.

Purpose beyond peer pressure.

SESSION 4 — Family & Community Bonds: Creating Accountability

Building strong relationships.

Family roles and support.

SESSION 5 — The Power of Saying No: Real-Life Training

Role-playing situations.

Practice saying "No" before temptation arises.

SESSION 6 — Community Rally: Public Stand for Change

Invite parents, leaders, officials.

Public commitments and celebration.

D. LEADER'S CHECKLIST

Before You Launch:

☐ Understand the full vision.
☐ Secure personal commitment.
☐ Gather core team.
☐ Secure location.
☐ Prepare materials and schedule.
☐ Promote launch event.

During the Program:

☐ Keep sessions focused and on schedule.
☐ Encourage participation and open dialogue.
☐ Provide mentorship and support.
☐ Build parent and youth relationships.

After the Program:

☐ Form ongoing support groups.
☐ Mentor new leaders.
☐ Evaluate and refine the program.
☐ Prepare to launch in new locations.

Printed in Dunstable, United Kingdom

77255379R00030